FVL
.00

Ascending
On the Ground

"Anyone who has ever tried to write about the spiritual journey knows how hard it is to find words that are big yet humble enough, serious yet light enough, full of drama and awe yet also stripped down and naked. This little book pulls it off. Jeff Brown has a most marvelous way with words—you think you're reading a joke, and it turns into a profound realization. Or you're following a complex thought to completion and suddenly it blossoms into a song and dance. I love learning about life and truth and love and purpose through the wizardry of Jeff's words. I think you will too."

—ELIZABETH LESSER, author of *Broken Open* and *The Seeker's Guide*; Cofounder, Omega Institute

"The book is fabulous—provocative, encouraging, and blazing with a clear-eyed truth that bows to no icons, only to the sweet, clear song of reality itself. There are enough sparks of wisdom in this book to ignite a blaze in the soul. Exhilarating, compassionate, in-sightful, these truth-soundings will vibrate in your being long after you have put them down. This is the kind of provocative companionship I cherish."

—PHILIP SHEPHERD, author of *New Self, New World: Recovering Our Senses in the Twenty-first Century*

"Jeff's writings are so inspiring! His quotes wisely and warmly support our shared expansion, and his Apologies series brings men and women together in a healing process that we all must go through to be whole. We heartfully recommend this special book."

—STEPHEN and ONDREA LEVINE, authors of *Embracing the Beloved* and *The Healing I took birth for*

"An insightful, wide-ranging collection of navigational aids for the path of awakening, with a special emphasis on grounded spirituality and deep healing."

—ROBERT AUGUSTUS MASTERS, author of *Spiritual Bypassing*, and *Transformation through Intimacy*

"*Ascending with both feet on the ground* is a concrete and vital approach to personal evolution. The process of "enrealment" is not for the faint of heart—this is a serious commitment to standing in the purifying fire of a deeply discerning and ever-expanding personal awareness. Jeff Brown's call to consciousness is clear and direct as he cuts to the heart of the matter with his words of wisdom in this eloquent and engaging book of quotes and commentary."

—FREEMAN MICHAELS, Co-host of *Cutting Edge Consciousness*

"Jeff Brown is the Spiritual Warrior our planet needs today. Truth permeates his work and his authentic "soul" message hugs my open heart. His wisdom will inspire you to not only take your step, but to reach the luminous place inside your soul."

—GRACE CIROCCO, author of *Take the Step, the Bridge will be There*

"This book is a breathtaking accumulation of offerings. It turns out that our greatest love affair is actually with our very own soul. With his written words and their subsequent echo through the center of the heart, Jeff Brown validates the inner journey, filled with both blustery canyons and snow-capped mountaintops, coupled with authentic external expression as the path to freedom. Rather than resist the paradoxes of life, we are invited to rest within them to know ourselves, full-out and full-on, as spirit-embodied. Savor each drop for this is as deliciously nitty-gritty as soul recognition gets!"

—ANNIE BURNSIDE, award-winning author of *Soul to Soul Parenting*

"This treasure of a book offers solid stepping stones on the road of possibility; paving the way for those who don't just want to meet God beyond their path, but *on* it."

—JESSICA BAHR, author of *The Awakening Woman*

Ascending with Both Feet On the Ground

Words to Awaken your Heart

Jeff Brown

TORONTO, CANADA

Published by Pipik Press
PO Box 64
Acton, Ontario
Canada L7J-2M2

Cover photo by Jeff Brown
Author photo by Paul Hemrend
Cover and book design by Susan Quasha
Printed in the USA

Some of the following quotes were previously published in *Soulshaping: Adventures in Self-Creation* (Pipik Press, 2007) and *Soulshaping: A Journey of Self-Creation* (North Atlantic Books, 2009).

Library and Archives Canada Cataloguing in Publication

Brown, Jeff, 1962–
Ascending with both feet on the ground : words to awaken your heart / Jeff Brown.
Issued also in electronic format.
ISBN 978-0-9808859-1-0
1. Self-actualization (Psychology). 2. Spiritual life. I. Title.
     BF637.S4B765 2012
     158 C2012-900220-8

This book is dedicated to my Facebook soulpod.

Thank you for your support.

We walk this journey together.

Preface

When my writing journey began in 2001, I was overwhelmed by a wave of language that flooded the banks of my consciousness. It was strong and it was determined, a soulnami of sacred purpose that absolutely had to be humanifest if I was to have any peace. When I resisted it, I lay sleepless in Toronto. When I honored it, I fell asleep, granted a little shut eye from the Divine Mother herself. Even when my shame and self-doubt obstructed the flow, I could feel the call to write right there, pushing up against the seams, readying for its next wave of expression. It was terrifying and it was beautiful and it was unstoppable. The nature of a calling once it has been awakened.

In the heart of writing *Soulshaping*, I constantly grappled with the meaning of grounded spirituality. I knew there was a model at the heart of the book, but I couldn't quite find it, perhaps because I wasn't yet grounded enough within myself. I had been tempted for years by everything ungrounded—the bliss trip, the head trip, the radical detachment trip. I loved the idea of finding the God-self independent of my pain-body and life's challenges. But no matter how hard I tried to find it there, I kept crashing back to earth with my baggage in tow. It became crystal clear that my unresolved emotional material was determined to be worked through, both to create more space inside for my callings to come to life and because my emotional debris was the karmic field where my soul's lessons were harvested. I couldn't mature in my spirituality without it. The gift of falling down.

Soon after publishing my original version of *Soulshaping,* I joined Facebook. At first, I didn't see any merit in it. It felt strange and isolating and oddly self-alienating. Projection Central. But I stayed with it, and it soon became clear that it was just what I needed. I began to work with my Facebook status, both as an opportunity to bring my writing to the world, and as a way of clarifying my perspective on grounded spirituality. My writing there became a kind of experiment, a way to play with concepts and ideas until they landed.

At some point, they landed. In the heart of playing with words, I stumbled upon a model of grounded spirituality that resonated with my experience and with my essential nature. The model—Ascending with both feet on the ground—is inclusive and embodied and honoring of all aspects of the sacred self. We are not just the light, or the mind, or the emptiness. We are not just what is comfortable and easy to digest. We are the everything. I call this *Enrealment*—the idea that a more 'heightened' consciousness is not all about the light (as enlightenment often implies) but is about becoming more real, more genuinely here in all respects—shadow and light, earth and sky, grocery list and unity consciousness. If non-duality means everything, it means that all aspects of the human experience are intrinsic to an expanded consciousness. It's all God, even the dust that falls off our awakening hearts. This philosophy is threaded through the following pages.

Perhaps my most profound experience on Facebook was a relational one. As any author will tell you, one of the great challenges of writing is the isolation. Some are well suited to it and welcome the opportunity to be left alone. I am not one of them. Although I feel the presence of the God-self when I write, I do miss human contact. Being alone in a room for hours on end has been one of my great challenges.

As I deepened in my commitment to Facebook as a forum for expression, a soulpod of wonderful beings gathered to support my journey and keep me company in the trenches of self-creation. In *Soulshaping*, I refer to the soulpod as "that person or group of people whom our soul finds the most resonance with at any given moment. It can include anyone that appears on our path to inform and catalyze our expansion – our biological family, significant figures, strangers with a lesson." On Facebook, I came into contact with a soulpod quite unlike any I had encountered before—a cadre of enheartened beings who shared my longing to both connect from the deep within and to support humanity in its liberation from the egoic ties that bind.

Over time, I came to love them and they became inextricably linked to my creative life. Time and again, they lit me up, carried me along, breathed air into my lungs when I needed it most. Just when I felt the most discouraged and drained by the challenges of writing, I would get an email that validated my efforts. Just when I would feel blocked in my efforts to clarify my own views of spirituality, an email dialogue with someone in the soulpod would crystalize my thinking. It always seemed to come at the perfect moment.

Their significance was never more obvious than in September, 2010, when I posted a note on my FB personal page called 'Apologies to the Divine Feminine (from a warrior-in-transition)'. Much to my surprise, this piece was met with a profound response, traveling from soul to soul rapidly, carried on the wings of a love by a soulpod heaven bent on supporting humanity. It was a humbling and startling opportunity to witness the magic of social media when it is benevolently intentioned. That piece and two subsequent gender writings (Apologies to the Sacred Masculine, The Awakening Man) are included at the back of this book.

With the right intention, social media is the perfect way to bridge to humanity and to work together to enhearten consciousness. Out in the world, the unconscious elements of the media can muffle our message, but in the insuppressible landscape of cyberspace, they cannot stop the soulnami of goodness from spreading. As we expand in connectiveness, we are laying down tracks for a more heartfelt, humane world. And we are beginning to see ourselves in each other, to recognize our shared humanness, to realize that we are walking beside each other on the trailways of transformation. Hands held together, hearts intertwined, bridging our way to God.

May we all look beyond our habitual frameworks of perception and imagine ourselves alight with unlimited possibility. There is a sacred purpose alive in each of us, a chaotic magnificence of epic proportions, a fire that will not die until it burns through our doubt and our shame and lights our way home.

With gratitude in my heart, I dedicate this book to my friends and supporters on Facebook, the wondrous gathering of souls who have stood behind my work as it has unfolded, in-couraging me to believe in my voice and message, sharing my writing heartfully and without agenda. I include among them Susan "Birdie" MacIver, a brilliant healer with a heart like no other, and two wonderful authors who have lovingly supported my own unfolding—Elizabeth Lesser, who suggested the sub-title for this book, and Oriah Mountain Dreamer, herself a master of grounded ascension. Such a magical collection of wing-lifters, lantern holders, and truth workers. Such a delight to walk beside you on the path. Blessings everywhere you step...

TORONTO, CANADA

August 9, 2012

Ascending with Both Feet
On the Ground

Essential lessons cannot be avoided. Callings don't go away. When we turn away from our lessons, when we ignore our truth-aches, the universe jumps into action, orchestrating our return—a symphony of self-creation dedicated to our unique expansion. This is the nature of karmic gravity—we are returned back to our path until we fully walk it. Return to sender, address now known...

Transcend Nothing,
Include Everything.

I imagine truth as a magnificent white-tipped Mountain. At its peak is a deeper and more inclusive experience of the moment. As we move through our lives, Truth Mountain comes in and out of view, calling out to us and reminding us of what is possible. The more truthful we are about our path, the higher our consciousness climbs. When our view is blocked, we know that we still have work to do in the valleys down below—traversing the foothills of illusion, sidestepping the quicksands of artifice, overcoming our fear of (interior) heights. But we will get to the peak, if we are willing to do the work, if we can be truthful with ourselves about the ways we avoid the truth.

Be especially wary of the judgmental on your spiritual journey, particularly those who are attached to practicalities at the expense of authenticity. Locked away in a symbolic prison (maximum 'security', no doubt) of their own making, they cling to the bars for dear life, afraid to taste the possibilities that wait on the other side. They may harp on your missed opportunities. They may tell you that life is entirely a question of survival—the best you can do is marry someone you don't deeply love, do work that does not deeply touch you, live a life of quiet desperation and frozen feeling. Don't listen to them—they have lost their light.

It's like we figure we are the only ones advocating for ourselves on this inner journey, but we aren't. We're not as alone as we think. While we are on the look-in, God is busily on the look-out for what will serve us. And then, when the moment is right, when we are truly ready to embrace our path, we walk right into the Godself on the bridge across forever, puzzled that we ever imagined ourselves separate.

I miss my heart when it closes.

I often feel that our greatest individual challenge is to close the gap between our unflattering self-concepts and the truth of our magnificence. To see ourselves through the eyes of those who love us. To love our so-called flaws as gifts from the Lords of Karma. Perhaps this is what we are here to do for those we care about—to hold a reflection of their divinity up before them until they are ready to embrace it as their own.

If All-Oneness is not built on a healthy regard for the rights, boundaries and magnificence of the individual soul, it's All-Nonsense. Grounded spirituality strikes a sacred balance between our experience of unity consciousness and our connection to true-path, that place where we feel both connected to the oneness and deeply connected to our divine purpose in the heart of it. The idea that we are 'All-One' takes on a whole new meaning when we interact with unity from an individuated and clarified purpose. There is the ocean of essence, and there is the individual droplet of meaning. Every soul has a vital role to play in this dance of sacred imagination.

There's no such thing as a fully realized master. That's just a hustle. We all have work to do. That's why we're here. To get a little closer...

If we don't know where we end and the other begins, we will have a difficult time establishing healthy connections. Those of us with weakly formed boundaries will be easily manipulated and influenced, often confusing our partner's feelings for our own. Those of us with firm boundaries will have a hard time opening our hearts to love. Our walls are simply too firm to penetrate. People with healthy boundaries tend to live somewhere in between. They have the capacity for vulnerability and self-protection at all times. When they do move toward one polarity, they do so with intentionality. In all cases, their sense of self remains intact.

There is so much suffering in the world. Sometimes I wonder how the earth holds it all. And then I see someone who has endured so much find their way through the pain tunnel to a truly better place. I am not talking about the bypassing of the pain-body. I am talking about the courageous working through of the emotional debris. And then I marvel at the human spirit, which creates whatever tools it needs to overcome the odds and find its way home. Wow. Humans. Wow.

Closing the heart is a self-fulfilling prophecy.
When we close it, we attract more reasons to keep
it closed. Opening the heart is a soul-fulfilling
prophecy. When we open it, we attract blessings:
Open-bless-a-me! Finally, blessings have a way in
and a way out to touch others. Try looking in the
mirror and repeating 'Open-bless-a-me' as a mantra,
an invitation to your higher self and to the universe
to bring blessings through the gateway of your heart.
OPEN-BLESS-A-ME!

When I look back at my life, I want to feel as though I have done all I can to honor my voice authentically. I am not concerned about how much money I have made, but, instead, how much karmic currency I have created. Karmic currency accumulates when we honor our path faithfully and share our inner riches with those we encounter. Let's open a joint account :)

You must never lose faith in your brilliance, no matter what the world sends your way. Your unique soul-scriptures live at the heart of you, lying in wait for their opportunity to be humanifest. They may be covered in dust, they may be hidden from view, but they are still in there, sparkling with infinite possibility.

The mythic life begins with our feet firmly planted on Mother Earth. We begin with the root chakra—the quest for Om begins at home—and we work our way up from there. Once the root chakra is satisfied, we proceed to the next chakras. As we heal and expand, there emerges a natural and sustainable movement upward, toward God. With our soles firmly planted, our soul has a leg to stand on in its efforts to go higher. From sole to soul—a sustainable connection to the Godself, one we can heartfully rely on.

It is important to grant yourself permission to wander as part of your spiritual journey. So often mischaracterized as lostness, there is a kind of immersion in the not knowing that is actually quite necessary if we are going to find our way home. So much information can come up when we are looking in no particular direction. By surrendering to the unknown, we create the space for a deeper knowing to emerge. In the heart of the not knowing, the paths that we are here to walk reveal themselves.

The monkey mind feeds on 'small peanuts': tireless anxieties, petty jealousies, fearful imaginings. Starve it by swimming in a vast ocean of delight.

Courage lives at the heart of this journey. We cling to the familiar and sometimes it kills us. We have to step beyond our comfort zone and make a leap of fate onto the growing edge of our soul. Faith in yourself is everything. "I am soul. I am vast. I have a right to fully honor my sacred purpose. I decide how far I go on this path. I am here for a reason, and I won't stop until I find it."

Love is my favorite sexual position.

The soulular phone connects your individual path to universal consciousness. Best thing about it is no set-up charges, no monthly bill, no ear infections from radiation. Just a free-speaking pipeline to divinity. The more inner work you have done to clear the lines, the clearer the connection. When it rings, be sure to answer it. It's the divine mother calling to remind you of why you are here.

Pierce the smokescreen of fearful indifference. Adventure heartily. Have faith in the shaping of what you cannot see.

Forgiveness is a beautiful thing, but it's essential that it arises organically. Many of us claim to have forgiven while still holding toxic emotions below the surface: the forgiveness bypass. The truth is that we cannot will ourselves into forgiveness. If we try to forgive before we have worked through the feelings, inauthenticity blocks our path. We cannot be in the real, because we're not emotionally real. Our heart is still back there.

There I was, paddling away in the heart of the main-stream, when a soulnami of truth rose up to meet me. Little did I know that my inner weaver had been working for years, spinning her web of karmic gold, transforming my consciousness while I slept, waiting for that just right moment to raise my authentic face from the emerging sea to stare me in the inner eye! Eegods!

The real journey is not one of adapting yourself to someone else's vision, but instead, shaping who you are with your own two hands. The karmic clay you work with lives deep inside your soul bones, awaiting your detection and expression. You are the sculptor of your own reality—don't hand your tools to anyone else.

God is an equal opportunity transformer. Everyone has access, everyone stands a chance. So long as we are willing to do the work necessary to clarify our inner channel, the universe will bring us boundless opportunities to shape our soul.

The School of Heart Knocks is an ongoing institution of higher learning. You don't get out until you're God.

There is such a fine line between relational passion and avoidant intensities. There were moments when my passionate nature was a direct reflection of my aliveness, but there were others when I was just using intensity and drama as a coping strategy, a way to actually hide from a deeper experience of the moment, some kind of addictive anti-mellow drama that procrastinated my relationship with reality. Somewhere below the drama was my real life, waiting in the wings to be lived. It was scary, but it called to me, reminding me that there is more to this life than a sidestepping of the inner world. There is the avoidant life, and then there is the one that is vulnerably true.

You're either in, or you're out. Sometimes it's that simple. No more stories, no more sidestepping, escape hatches, veiled retreats. You're either in, or you're out.

I am (also) my body.

The soul has a no-return policy. Once we cross a certain point in our expansion, we can't go back. As we honor our calling, we grant it more space inside of us. Light begets light—at a certain point, there is no way to escape the inner beacon. Our calling begins to soak every aspect of our lives, whatever the cost or inconvenience. We cannot live without our call because our call has become us. Path decisions then come straight from the heart of true-path, and we move only when our soul motor tells us to. Turn on your karmic engine…

We have to continue to close the gap between the world as it is and the world as it ought to be. This is the work of all spiritual warriors—to clear the path of debris, to infuse the path with so much truth that others can find their way home. Truth workers united under the banner of authentic self-revealing!

PUBLIC SERVICE ANNOUNCEMENT!

Due to the cumulative effect of collective sharing and loving intentionality, the Shame Train has derailed at the junction of Self-Belief and Divine Uniqueness. The engine couldn't run on self-hatred any longer. All formerly shamed passengers please disembark the train. You are free. A new train— fueled by healthy self-regard and sacred purpose— will be along momentarily to pick you up. No tickets required on this self-love train—just a growing faith in your sacred magnificence. All aboard!

A true master follows her own footprints, encoded within her before arriving in this incarnation. Someone else may remind her, someone else may in-power her, but no one else can possibly know the unique contours of her own true-path. Since you are the only one living in your temple, only you can know its scriptures and interpretive structure. The next step is right there inside you, divinely imprinted on the souls of your feet.

Excessive analysis perpetuates emotional paralysis.

Shame is rooted in the shame pit of generations before, perpetuating the self-hatred of the collective unconscious, still lodged in dark energies and imaginings. Your shame has nothing to say about who you really are, never did, never will. In truth, you don't need anyone else's permission to be here. God gave you all the permission you need. And who are you really? A divinely intended wave of magnificence, an ocean of gifts just waiting to be opened, a soulnami of epic proportions. First we clear the path of inner debris, then we walk our way home...

I hear all the doomsayers, but I believe we've entered into a time of great promise. I don't believe the world will dissolve in the coming years or that we're facing ultimate financial collapse. We'll have challenges, but we'll work them out. I believe that people of sacred purpose are more necessary now, not because tragedy is upon us, but because we're moving beyond survivalism as a guiding principle. We are moving, side by side, heart in heart, towards authenticity as our shared way of being. Of course it's gonna get noisy as egoic walls come tumbling down, of course the energy is going to intensify and frighten us. It comes with the territory. But we will make it through, we just will. We're brilliantly adaptive, and on the deepest truest levels, we all want to lay down our arms, and move through life from the heart outward. We may be able to endure most anything, but we are built to love.

You can look for a relationship, but you can't look for love. Love finds you when it's ready.

As it turns out, life actually isn't a dress rehearsal. It's an undress rehearsal. We come down here time and time again to practice shedding our ego armor until we can step on the stage of eternity, naked and exposed before God, as God. Exit, cloud left...

Kindness melts defenses. Kindness softens edges.
Kindness pierces armour. Kindness eradicates shame.
Kindness lightens loads. Kindness awakens hope.
Kindness clears debris. Kindness invites connection.
Kindness opens hearts. Kindness bridges souls.
Kindness inspires kindness. Let us always be kind.

Although you may think that your sacred purpose is way ahead of you on the path, it's actually just sleeping inside of you. It will appear now and then, like a butterfly floating behind your eyes, rehearting you of what lives inside of you. You may not see it often, but it always has you in its sights.

I am learning how to hold my own hand. They forgot to teach that in primary school. I had to go to the School of Heart Knocks to learn that.

Sometimes the path of courage is a quiet one, traveling in its own subtle ways along the corridors of the inner world.

I am imagining the key players in our lives as faces in a deck of playing cards—Karmic faceball cards. All the players essential to the game of life are there—token villains, benevolent healers, dear friends. When we look a bit deeper, we see all the archetypes and aspects intrinsic to our wholeness staring right back at us. There they are, there we are, all together now. Ah, we were on the same team after all...

All too often, the positive thinking movement becomes a bypass of reality, a skimming of the surface of our inner lives. Too many have followed this approach to transformation and lost their way, making major life changes without the ground to support them. Don't be intoxicated by the allure of wish-full thinking. Instead, focus your energy on genuine foundation building, doing the painstaking work to clear the inner channel and learn essential lessons so that your quest for true-path is solid and true. Divine Perspiration begets Divine Inspiration. The universe responds to authentic change—nothing feigned will do.

Success is simply the completion of a soul-step, however unsightly it may be. You have finished what you started when the lesson is learned. What an egoic and fear based culture calls a wonderful opportunity may be fruitless and misguided for the soul. If you need to explore ten careers in order to excavate and honor your unique true-path, then so be it. It's your path to walk. Flake it till you make it!

You have to acknowledge yourself as a victim before you can recognize the karmic choices that you made to become one. It's essential that you honor and work through the emotions and memories associated with what you have been through. But when you move beyond that, and see yourself as grower and choice-maker, you enter a whole new realm of self-*in*powerment. Blame is just a short-term way station. The ultimate step is soul responsibility...

I am not interested in enlightenment if it means detachment from the emotional body, the earth plane, the challenges of being human. I am interested in enrealment, because it means that my most spiritual moments are inclusive, arising right in the heart of all that is human: joy and sorrow, shopping list and unity consciousness, fresh mangos and stale bread. Enrealment is about living in all aspects of reality simultaneously rather than only those realms that feel the most comfortable. We are not just the light, or the mind, or the emptiness, or perpetual positivity. We are the everything. It's ALL God, even the dust that falls off my awakening heart.

Go shuck yourself!

Caught between a rock and a heart place, I am trusting the universe to bring me through the openings...the just right karmic crevice, the crack in the heart where the rivers of truth flow through. Ah, to continue to be a canoeist of the heart, riding the rapids of a growthful consciousness, coming to rest on the tender shores of my own essence. I mean, isn't that the harbour we seek?

It took years to realize that I could acknowledge that a wrongdoer was doing their best, given their own context, and that I still had every right to move the anger I was holding from their actions. I thought that because I knew where they were coming from, it wasn't okay to acknowledge their impact. But it's about holding both awarenesses at once. Maybe they were doing their best, but we still have to work through their effects.

We must be under no illusion that all soul mates are meant to last a lifetime. Some are only meant to last a moment. That brief soul gaze with a 'stranger' at the grocery store that reminded you of your own essence was just right. That unexpected weekend encounter that set your spirit to soar is perfect. That great love that walked away after cracking your heart open was just what the soul doctor ordered. Whatever you need to smooth the rough diamond of the soul. No matter how long they last, profound connections paint pictures of possibility in the sky, expanding our lens for all eternity.

Spiritual growth is so much the artist's journey. Our inner world is soul art, our lives its heartfelt canvas. Like true artists, we have to find that delicate balance between willfulness and surrender—when to act, when to still. We have to allow our form to change as intuition demands. Home is where the art is. Chaotic Magnificence…

It's never rude to interrupt your false-self.

Real presence comes through the open heart. You cannot heal and resolve your emotional material with your mind. Your emotional material does not evaporate because you watch it. You can only heal your heart with your heart.

I am a recovering addict—addicted to artifice, disguise, misidentification, distraction, substitute gratifications, materialism, being right, winning every silly battle. Now I want to be a re-uncovering addict—addicted to baring my naked soul for all to see, particularly me. I want to see straight through my armor to the essential being quivering below. Nothing to hide, no place to hide it.

Don't wait until your death bed to finally open your inner eye, safe in the knowledge that your vulnerability is time-limited. Better to inwaken now.

I looked for God on the skyways of self-avoidance, but she wasn't there. The bliss-trip floated me away, the head-trip blocked my heart, the radical detachment trip was oddly robotic. I went down this road for some time, seemingly joyous on the outside, but a bubbling cauldron of unresolved feelings and memories in the deep within. I actually found God in my heart. There she was, in my grief, in my ecstasy, in my awakening heart. Hearty, heart heart…

If only I knew then, what I don't know now.

If we just accept, that even on our best day, we have only gone a short distance down the path to wholeness, we will not fall into the trap of taking ourselves too seriously. The School of Heart Knocks loves teachers who remain students.

At the heart of our expansion is the capacity to be vulnerable again. Although the world rewards insensitivity with the spoils of war, it takes more courage to surrender than to numb. I am not talking about a weakened form of surrender, but one that is emblazoned with courage. It is through our vulnerable, open heart that our divinity rises up to meet us. So often the most 'damaged' people are the most advanced and feeling souls. They feel everything and are more strongly impacted by the disparity between an authentic life and the falsified energy of the world. We must never surrender our right to surrender.

One of the great challenges of finding your sacred purpose is that it shines a light to those areas of your life that are not alight with the same vibration. When the soul is on fire, it burns through everything that doesn't truly resonate with it, leaving only karmic ash in its wake. This is the up-framing nature of a growthful path—that which distracts us from the path, that which doesn't share our new resonance, must be shed so that we can continue to evolve. It's not always easy to say farewell to relationships and familiar ways of being, but it comes with the territory...

I just saw God drive by on her bicycle, sliding a little on the wet road. God got off her bike, and started to walk it along the sidewalk. She seemed to prefer to feel her feet on the ground.

There is a time to adventure heartily into new possibilities, but there is also a need for quiet integration time on the self-creation journey. We can have all the peak experiences we want but the real work happens between the peaks, while laying down and integrating on the valley floor. Growers are inch worms. Lasting transformation is an incremental process, one soul-step at a time. This may frustrate us, but it's the only way to craft an awareness that is authentic and sustainable.

The body is far more than just a vessel for the soul. It is the field where the soul's lessons are harvested. It is the breeding ground for the soul's emergence. *Repressed emotions are unactualized spiritual lessons.* In order to grow in our spirituality, we must bring our joy and our suffering through our emotional body until our lessons are birthed. We must 'cell our soul.'

Your inner knowing. Don't leave home without it.

I just witnessed another person in authority talking down to someone needlessly. Perhaps we should develop a program for anyone in a position of authority. ERT (Ego Reduction Training) would include a strong emphasis on therapeutic process and witness-awareness, so that people in power know their stuff, recognize their projections, and learn to communicate in the kindest way possible. If we can raise their consciousness and strengthen their inner-authority, they can move from the heart outward in their interactions with humanity. Let's make ERT humandatory.

Love is God in her most clarified forms.

I find this whole judgment around where individuals should be at by a certain stage of their life ridiculous. Only the soul knows the path it is here to walk, what it has overcome, which achievements to measure its progress by. Nobody knows why you are here, except you. You're the only one that can find that. People judge as though they have it all figured out, but their judgments often just smokescreen their own confusion. Are we late bloomers, or on-time growers? This is a personal decision. The important thing is that we keep on walking towards a place that feels like home.

There is a fine line between humble and ashamed. Humble opens the door to God. Shame closes it. If we move through our lives riddled with shame, we have a much harder time believing in our inherent magnificence. Unfortunately, many of us do not have self-love handed to us. We have to forge it ourselves in the fires of life. This is the work of our lives, recognizing the Godself sleeping at the core of our being.

It's not all falling apart. It's all coming together.

You should be more afraid of avoiding your path than walking it.

Truth is the gateway to the moment.

Beginner's mind doesn't do it for me. Its beginner's heart I seek—the freshness of appreciation that comes through the open heart. Got a few more clearings to do first—some old primal stuff I wasn't ready for yet—and some heart-core lessons to learn—I can see their shape off in the distance, calling me to get on with it—and then maybe, by the grace of the inner knower, beginner's heart will arise. I spy with my inner eye ... a purer heart waiting around the karmic bend.

Friends fell away as I individuated on my soul's journey. As I shed one self-sense, I no longer identified with the people attached to it. Old ways of interacting seemed artificial, scripted, silly. Whereas before it was fine to hang out and waste time, now there was no time to lose. Now I had to protect my sacred purpose from connections that undermined it

Be prepared for the lonely times on the journey. It can be very isolating to quest for true-path amid the trumpets of modern life. Walking through uncharted territory often means walking alone. This is particularly true in the transition stages before we find our consciousness soulpod. It's like primary school all over again—who will be my first REAL friends?

It's very difficult to close the heart after it has opened to God's glory. The open heart twinkles the name of God.

I am in-countering terrorism of a shaming form. Ah, the inner terrorist. There he is, standing before me with his usual weaponry (disdain, despair, dogma), blocking the path home. I am quite habituated to succumbing to his shaming style, but this afternoon, I am looking the bastard in the inner eye, daring him to come a little closer. When he gets within reach, I am going to give him the hug he has been longing for since time immemorial. Maybe, just maybe, I can melt him with kindness.

In so many love relationships, there seems to be a runner (someone who is more aloof) and a chaser (someone who is more eager to connect). Often these are established patterns—some of us tend to either chase or flee in every relationship—but not always, as many of us have fears in both directions (the fear of abandonment, and the fear of being engulfed) and live out both patterns at various times. As we heal our wounds, we shed these patterns, and get more comfortable with being with only those that meet us on equal footing—eye to eye, heart to heart. That's when the real vulnerability begins.

Let's not throw the entire ego out with the bath water. I'm not talking about the unbridled ego, the narcissistic ego, the imbalanced ego. I'm talking about the strong self-concept, the boundaried sense of self, the healthy ego that helps us to manage reality and honor our purpose. Without a strong sense of self, we don't have the solidity to sustain the journey. Without a solid core, our forays into unity come crashing back to earth. Solid me, solid we...

It is important to realize that it is possible to hold the belief in someone's highest possibilities while simultaneously accepting that they are not at a stage where a friendship is appropriate. Because growth-oriented individuals tend to be empathic, they run a particular risk of remaining close to people who can drag them down. If two people cannot meet on relatively equal footing, there are two options: the relationship can end, or it can be organized around the developmental stage of the least conscious member. Give yourself permission to go where the growth is. Some of us are meant to jump through karmic hoops together, some of us aren't...

The only illusion is that this is an illusion. It's as real as real gets.

I have finally found my guru—my toes, my feet, my hips, my hands, my heart. What a thing to imagine our guru as intrinsic to who we are rather than external to our embodied experience. If we really listen to the body, its truth-aches will remind us when we are walking in the wrong direction, its truth-chills will remind us when we are walking our true-path. Thousands of years of knowing in our body temple, eternal wisdom as to directionality. No need to attach to anyone else's knowing. We are living in a castle of awareness. The Body of God.

Your lack of readiness is an illusion communicated by shame-ridden parts of you that will forever have you believing that you have to take a few more steps until your real life begins. It's an illusion of epic proportions. Get to it brilliant being. There is no need to procrastinate the gateway to wholeness—it stands before you with your name on it. The world is ready for what you have to offer. No time like the presence.

It is essential that we step out beyond our habitual range of e-motion and create new pathways of possibility on the journey. We don't get anywhere if we stay stuck in the same ole' groove. May you find the courage it takes to leave behind well-trodden paths, the faith to open new doors in the heart of the emptiness, the persistence necessary to push beyond your comfort zone. Lost is intrinsic to found. May your sense of wander lead you home.

Sometimes those who seem impossible to awaken, are actually doing invisible prep work.

We may not be only our stories, but we also are our stories. If we stay connected to the fact that our story has both a localized *and* a universal dimension, we are on the right path. Not identifying ourselves as our story, but identifying the juice at the heart of our story as fundamental to our expansion. In the heart of our stories are the personal identifications and unresolved issues that are the grist for our spiritual expansion. Never throw the story out with the bath water. Without karmic clay to work with, our expansion is stalled. God is a dish best served juicy.

Today, I drove my weary bones to the country. I walked into the woods, feeling the armor and tightness I have accumulated these last months. I had returned to warrior, so familiar. I got down on my knees by the river of essence, renewing my commitment to the Divine Mother and her heartfelt ways, kissing the ground she walks on. The armor, it clanged to the ground. Time to surrender, sang the birds of pray.

Quick fix,
Loooooooong suffering.

It is seldom as simple as asking the universe for what we want and we get it. We need to get our emotional world consistent with our requests before they will be taken seriously by the universe. The more emotionally unresolved we are, the denser the message we transmit. The trick is to clear ourselves out from the inside-out so that we are emanating from a clear and unified channel. Then our request might carry more weight, then it might fall on open ears...

This whole dance is one of sacred imagination, envisioning the next set of eyes we will see the world through, and then doing the work to humanifest it. At first we only see a faint light way ahead on the path. Then we see an etch-o-sketch of unlimited possibility, first one form, then another, until we craft a shape that is deeply true. Take out your paint brush and paint yourself into being.

Dear Jesus, I am sorry that we confused presents with presence. So silly of us.

Imagine the next step, one where we don't see relationship endings as defeats, but as victories and necessary openings on the path to wholeness. Imagine the next step, where we honor the courage it took to open to the possibility of love, where we see intimacy as a wondrous opportunity to deepen in karmic stature. How can it ever be a complete defeat? It took such courage to brave it all, to make love with the divine, to touch God through our vulnerable heart. This is not to say that we don't grieve loss, but to remind us of the opportunity that lives at the heart of every farewell. A little scar tissue can go a long way on the path to presence.

Empty yourself, and what waits in the wings will fill the space.

Honor your inner champion, the one that chooses to confront and work through your obstacles to wholeness, the one that slays the inner dragons with tenderness and persistence. Isn't it time that we soulebrated the courage it takes to confront our patterns time and again? Isn't it time for an up-framing of our often negative view of our challenges? Instead of "oh no, not that pattern again", how about recognizing that we are CHAMPIONS for simply taking them on? How about seeing ourselves as some of the first humans with the blessed opportunity to shift the negative patterning intrinsic to the collective unconscious? We are PIONEERS, for God's sake! What a fantastic thing—to be pioneers in the inner world! Every little step is a radical paradigm shift for humanity.

If you want to star gaze, no need to wait for the night. Just look in the mirror anytime—there's a whole star-lit network of divine possibility staring right back at you. The inner universe is where it's at, the galaxy of golden possibility that lives right inside your soul-skin. It just takes a little imagination to see it, but then, WOW! You never looked so Go(o)d.

It gets easier the more evidence you get that your inner knowing was right all along. At first, trusting a hint or a whisper of true-path, and then, a slight breeze against your cheek, inviting you in a new direction. This is the hard phase, when you have yet to validate your intuition with actual experience. This is when you need to hang tight and do everything possible to keep your faith afloat. Eventually, the inner message becomes more direct, more seamless, indistinguishable from your very breath. That's when you have become your intuition. That's when you find true-path everywhere you step. The bridge that gets you from faith to certainty is built with heartfelt determination.

Love is kind. It doesn't matter what we feel down below, it matters how we humanifest those feelings. Love is kind. If it's unkind, it's not love.

In most cases, the guru is just a travel agent for the particular trip that helped him to become more aligned. He is talking to himself, reminding himself of what he most needs to remember. With only rare exceptions, he cannot tell us our truth. He cannot tell us what to know. The most he can do is call out to our knowing and remind us of what we inherently knew all along. Anything else is usually a misappropriation of karmic funds. Be careful.

For me, happiness is being true to path, even if I feel miserable :).

I am cozying up to my pain-body this morning and thanking it for its presence. It doesn't want me to trip out of it. It wants me to nourish it and honor its wisdom. I mean, where would we be without our shadow? What would grow us? Not to glorify the challenges of life, but I expanded in my spirituality through a deepening interface with my shadowy material. Shadow as karmic fodder, Shadow as grist for the soul mill...

If you can be in heartbreak, and keep your heart totally open, you are living very close to God.

It's wonderful to have gratitude in your attitude, so long as you genuinely feel it. If not, stop the lies, and get in touch with how you are really feeling.

In a mad dash to react away from the perils of anger, we went too far and lost a key piece of the emotional integrity and expression cycle. Anger is a legitimate emotion that signals that a person has been violated. By discouraging and shaming it, we actually disrupt natural emotional rhythms and encourage inauthentic ways of being. In addition, repressing the emotions simply keeps the anger alive. The negativity goes underground, manifesting in a myriad of destructive forms, including passive aggressiveness, self-destructive behaviour and all manner of disease. It is one thing to discourage the inappropriate expression of anger, but let us not throw the whole process out with the bath water. There is a place for healthy anger in an evolving world.

The faster we run, the more determined is the Universe to slow us down. The more embedded our methods of self-distraction, the more agitating the truth-aches calling us back to authenticity. The more eagerly we race to the sky, the more intense the lessons that bring us back to earth. The universe has no interest in our flight from reality. It wants us right here. Nowhere else...but here.

It all comes down to truth—truth *or* consequences.

It is important to recognize that to live in a continuous state of detachment is to do the spiritual bypass and miss the moment altogether. It is to trip out of the body that carries the karmic seeds for our transformation. It is to leave earth before our time. To be sure, there are times when detachment is necessary: when we need to be reminded of something beyond our localized perceptions, when we need a peek into a vaster reality, when we need to distinguish between that which serves us and that which derails us. Indeed, we are far more than our monkey mind, our neurotic patterns, our unimaginative lens. But perpetual detachment is self-avoidance masquerading as enlightenment. At some point we have to come back down into our body and work with what lives inside us.

If you can't trust your soul, who can you trust?

When we dunk our hearts in the river of essence,
we come back up for air with new eyes.

I love humanity and have so much faith that we will co-create a world that reflects our heartfelt magnificence. Despite our blind spots, growing pains and harsh lessons, we are love. Everything else, disguises. I know it looks bleak sometimes, but we are an unstoppable force of (good) nature that cannot be stopped. We have many more challenges to come, but we are going to find our way through them. Our spirits are just so beautiful. We won't rest until all the shrouds fall away, and we are exposed as the heart beings that we are. Such love, such love…

Grace is not something that pours down from the heavens. It is something that rises up from within us.

You can't skip steps on the self-creation journey. If you step on the right path at the wrong time, you have stepped on the wrong path. When you jump to certain stages too early, you get pulled back by lack of preparation. You have to go through the stages intrinsic to your unique true-path. Everything at its own pace, one soulbeat at a time.

We are each so brilliant, so gifted, libraries of unlimited possibility, soul-scriptures waiting for us on every inner shelf. Reach inside and take a good firm hold of your magnificence.

When you walk through the gateway of your sacred purpose, you walk into yourself. Like the great wall of karma, it protects you from unconscious forces and holds your process safe. Blessingly buffered from the madness of the world, your purpose filters out those relationships and energies that undermine your expansion. Infused with vitality and a clarified focus, new pathways of possibility appear where before there were obstacles. Life still has its challenges, but you interface with them differently, coated in an authenticity of purpose that sees through the veils to what really matters. The rivers of essence rise up to meet you, carrying you from one wave of expansion to another...

We often talk about living in the moment but it is my experience that we cannot live fully in the moment if we are not living in truth. Without truth, our breaths are somehow incomplete, our presence shrouded, our intimacy half-hearted because we are not fully there for it. The moment we own our truths, we get truth-chills — little sighs of relief from our body temple — as the veils to clarity fall away and our divine presence enters. Here we are. Here now.

Sensitivity is a sign of life. Better hurt than hardened. I bow to those who keep their hearts open when it is most difficult, those who refuse to keep their armor on any longer than they have to, those who recognize the courage at the heart of vulnerability. After all the malevolent warriors end each other, the open-hearted will inherit the earth.

In a survivalist world, it is rare for anyone to even identify his or her calling. Most of us barely ever scratch the itch. When you have the chance to actualize them, you have to try, because you are not doing it for yourself alone. You are also doing it for all the members of your soulpod, alive and dead. If you complete your task, however small or humble it may be, you take them all to the next level. We expand together...

It doesn't matter how much two people love one another if they are developmentally incompatible, or if there is not a shared willingness to become conscious. This is why they call it a relationship instead of a loveship. Love alone is not enough. If you want it to last, you have to relate to each other in ways that keep the ship afloat.

The only real homeland security is the knowledge that whatever the world brings your way, your soul is safe in your own two hands. A certain faith develops, not simply that the universe will provide for you, but that *you* will provide for you. They can shame you, they can obstruct you, but they can no longer alienate you from your own essence.

Let's take ourselves out from under the collective bushel of shame, and worship at our temple of humanness—the one staring at us in the mirror. No averting of the eyes, no shallow gaze, just look at God's wondrous creation as she is. Melt the shame with presence. We have been conditioned to honour ourselves only when we actualize our highest standards but the shift comes when we honour ourselves in our (seeming) imperfection, warts and all. A new spiritual practice—to love ourselves at our mucky worst, to pray to our humanity in all its shadowy forms, to kiss the hand that feeds you. It's all God, isn't it? How can it be any other way?

Depression is frozen feeling. The mystery begins with our history. Although the physical body travels forward chronologically, one's emotional consciousness always lingers at any point of departure. Before we can fully surrender to the mystery, we have to go back and heal the wounds and memories that obstruct us. This is the 'power of then.' We've got to *be there then*, before we can *be here now*.

Keep the faith and the faith will keep you.

I don't believe in rising above anything. I believe in living it through the bones of my being.

There is a wondrous high-way to wholeness living inside you. The more deeply you trust your instincts as to path, the more often the high-way will rise up to meet you.

The only one you need to answer to is staring at you in the mirror. Does s(he) feel good about your efforts, your achievements, your intentionality, your way of moving through the world? Does s(he) say YES when you ask if you are making progress in a challenging world? If so, then who cares what anyone else thinks? There are lite-dimmers everywhere—ignore them, and come back to your inner knowing.

We have nothing to hide, and nowhere to hide it. It just takes so much energy to bury our truth, and what can we reveal that hasn't been other's experience anyway? Our secrets aren't that unique. They are intrinsically human. Let's practice the arts of radical transparency & shameless self-admission. Imagine truth circles in every community... "I admit..." and then we dance.

There is nothing but brightly lit, unstoppably beautiful, soulgasmic, heart-opening, tear-inducing, armor softening, dance inspiring, God honoring, love-awakening magnificence lurking below your adaptations and disguises. Grab a noisy shovel and dig yourself out.

Be Real Now.

Befriend your confusion. Don't be fooled by its chaotic appearance—confusion is a sign that your soul is in transition. Welcome it as a friend that has come from far away to bring you home. Be open to it. Keep it close.

Not a day goes by when I don't feel challenged and distracted by an old pattern, another test, a false-path that holds temptation. I don't think it's a simple question of finding our sacred purpose and owning it every moment. I think we are always pulled off of it and have to remember. Forget, remember, forget, remember. It's just that the remembering gets easier over time.

It will take more than a change of thinking. It will also require a healing of the collective heart.

Bringing our soul lessons through takes more than awareness. It is an active process that demands a courageous willingness to live our experiences right through to completion. This means staying with our feelings until they are truly done with us, no matter how uncomfortable they are. It will be difficult at times, but the feelings will only hurt until they convert into the lessons at their heart. Although we may not see it at first, there is a method to our sadness.

I honor my fellow soul travelers who self-identify as light workers, but I prefer to identify myself as a truth worker. Love the light, to be sure, but more interested in focusing on how we come into the light. It doesn't happen in a karmic vacuum. For me, excavating and honoring my truths is my path to the light. Truth as source, truth as en-light-ener, truth as doorway to the moment. Fellow truth-workers unite!

This idea that we have to have it all figured out by a certain age is a societally induced prison that ignores the depths and meaning of the human incarnation, which is about authenticity and growing towards wholeness and not about meeting a deadline. Better to honor our path faithfully than imprison ourselves with a time-line. Timelessness is where it's at, one growth-full step at a time.

Ignore everything that doesn't serve the honoring of your purpose.

You are beautifully enough. Your stories of 'not good enough' are fictional novels written by a culture still hiding its light under a bushel of shame. The REAL story, your TRUE autobiography, is one of inherent magnificence, courage and divinity flowing through your soul-veins. So you decide which book to read—the fictional novel written by those who do not SEE you, or the HOLY BOOK written by your glorious spirit.

So many of us have defined ourselves and made our path decisions by adapting our identities to the structures outside of us. The next step is adapting our structures to who we really are.

With all due respect to the School of Heart Knocks—hardship as a vehicle for growth—we ought to never forget pleasure as a path. Are you hearing me, Divine Mother? We want to curl up on your karmic lap and learn some happy lessons too.

We may have to work hard to bring it to light, but we must never give up on our profound nature. Below the surface, we are all sacred dynamite, waiting for that just right spark to ignite our divine purpose. Once ignited, we explode into particles of unlimited possibility. What seemed profound before becomes just the tip of the soulberg. When you are ready, look inside and your magnificence will rise to the surface on the wings of the inner dove. I tell you, it's that close...

Perhaps the hardest thing about the path is that it's entirely up to us how far we go, how deep we go, how authentic we become. No one else can do it for us—it's all ours, it's the art of self-creation, it's adult responsibility. It's such a private decision we come back to time and again—Am I willing to do the work to find and to live my path? Do I have the faith, courage and persistence I need to keep getting back up off the ground when things go awry? How badly do I want an authentic life? What price am I willing to pay to create one?

Lasting transformation is a slow winged process, one little flutter at a time. Profound experiences can accelerate the journey, but much of the real change happens at slower paces and the places in between. Changing the migratory direction of your soul is a lifelong process.

You are not your shame, your fears, your addictions, your games, your guilt. You are not your resistance to your true path. You are not your self-doubt. You are not your self-distraction patterns. You are not your escape hatches. You are not your pessimism about a life of meaning and purpose. You are not here merely to survive and endure. You are sacred purpose. You are here to embody God.

Let's do the GodDance.

Look in the mirror and enjoy the light show.

Change happens from the truth out.

The very fact that we are trying to heal our hearts in a world where so many have had to bury their hurt is already extraordinary. It may not seem like such a big deal, but when the energy has been moving in another direction for so many generations, it is quite a challenge to turn the tide. We are breaking new inner ground, after all. Recognizing this should translate into giving ourselves a break when we can't quite get it perfect. It's a long path back to the receptive heart, one opening at a time...

Soulitude isn't easy, but somewhere at its core is a map, an inner travelogue of the paths we are here to wander. Sometimes those paths have tangible markers, sometimes they are perfectly hazy and quiet like. We lose patience with path too easily in this substitute gratification culture. Hang in there, in the space between the knowings.

I am an over-cover agent for the divine. I like this kind of in-visible espionage, inviting seemingly warring archetypes into sacred balance. Lets' form a new kind of CIA—the Core Intuition Agency— where we work to in-power and elevate the inner knowing, where we bring all voices of truth into divine communion, where we remind others of their sacred magnificence. Top Not-Secret!

We fall down, we get up. We get up, we fall down. We either see our stumbles as examples of our own victimhood—we are being abused by the universe—or as opportunities for self-creation—embracing life's challenges as essential lessons from the Godself within. The gift of falling down—there's gold in them there spills. Stumbling toward ecstasy...

Some say, 'Do what you love and the money will follow.' This is a misleading aphorism that only applies to some. 'Do what you love and the money *may* follow' is more realistic. Some of us follow a path that does not generate an adequate income on its own, but we are called to follow it nonetheless. We have to do what we came here to do even if it means that we make our money doing something else.

I never made any progress on the path when I compared myself to others. Someone was always ahead of me, and most of what I saw in them was projection anyway. I made real progress when I became my own benchmark, when I actively compared my humanifestation to where it was the day before—Am I little closer to where I want to be today? Have I become a little kinder, a little less distracted, a little more connected to my callings? Am I a little more at home in my skin? Do I feel more at peace with path?

If we do what we really love, there is no such thing as retirement. The soul beat goes on. If we love our work, we may well make less money before sixty-five, but we are much more likely to live longer and healthier, and to actually want to continue working. Is wholeness not the only retirement plan worth saving for?

The monkey mind is not the source of our anxiety. It's a symptom of it. The anxiety emanates from a constricted emotional body. We have to wake down the body, before we can wake up our awareness. The body is not simply the karmic vehicle that drives the mind from one lesson to another. It is the heart of the matter, the soul's garden of truth. A built-in authenticity-mometer, the body dulls when we are living falsely, and glows when we are true to path. If we don't tend to the garden, there will be no place to pray.

Practice the art of selective attachment, the process of sifting everything through an essential filter, connecting only to those experiences and relationships that support your true-path. Kind of like a heart with a gate at the opening, it creaks open only when you make the conscious decision to unlatch the gate and welcome in the next lesson on your path. If something supports your ascension, bring it on. If it doesn't, stay away.

I want to help create a world where everyone's authentic self is invited, excavated & revered. A world where you are loved for being whoever the f**k you are, where we grok that every soul is divinely intended, where our shame has melted in the presence of mutual respect, where we bow down to each other's uniqueness. Not just 'I am that, too' but also 'I love what is unique about you'. Yah, that's the golden ticket.

It is so beautiful what happens when we define relationship success solely in terms of whether we have learned from it, expanded from it, grown to the next stage on our spiritual journey. When we move from this perspective, relationship becomes a wonderful depth charge for our own healing and expansion. If we find a lifelong partner-great!—but if we don't, we get better at partnering with our inner lover.

Finding your way home requires a spirit of adventure. It does not mean that you always have to do. It means that whatever you are doing, or not doing, is experienced as a spiritual inquiry, an information gathering, an active exploration of reality. Sitting still can be a profound adventure if you are present and inquisitive.

Inner growth is like a truth serum that reframes and clarifies our lens to the outside world. Our social life is one of the things that must change to accommodate our expansion. In this process, we must have faith that we will survive that often-lonely space between old friends falling away and new ones showing their face. This faith is our buffer against the temptation to go back to the familiar. If we can hang tight and make conscious efforts to connect, the next soulpod will be walked in our direction when the moment is right. We call to them, they call to us, and our angels broker the deal.

Love it forward.

If there is anything to get used to on this path, it is repetition of pattern. The fall back to habitual ways is a natural part of the journey home. Like turtles, we stick our head out until it becomes too uncomfortable, and then we retreat to the safety and familiarity of our shell. The time we spend under the shell can be just what we need to integrate new experiences into our usual ways of being. So long as we persist in sticking our head back out a little further each time, we continue to grow. Three steps forward, two steps back, is still progress.

If we don't embrace our confusion, we remain trapped between worlds—on the one hand, old ways of being ready to die; on the other, new ways of being eager to be born. By holding the space for all the possibilities at once, clarity emerges on its own terms. The bridge from one side to the other is confusion. We must learn how to cross it on the way home.

Dear Body... Thank you for being my authenticity-mometer, my temple of truth. How beautifully you carried my sacred purpose until I was ready for the hand-off. You reminded me with truth-chills whenever I walked in the right direction. You tripped me up with truth-aches whenever I dared to walk in someone else's shoes. What is so remarkable is that you never failed to communicate with me when I was living a lie. I may not have been ready to listen, but you never abandoned your faith in my possibilities. I now know that my true-path is encoded in the bones of my being. Not a temple that I visit, but one that I am.

When we are ready to stop turning a blind eye to the meaning of our experiences, we tune in to the learning channel as a way of being. Through this lens, expectations are meaningless: soul gifts come in unexpected packaging. Seeming failures can be welcome events—sometimes the ego suffers while the soul rejoices. We are knocked to the ground on the Earth plane but tripped up spiritually. The ladder to heaven is made from broken rungs.

Praises to those who stand by others when the going gets tough, when the body is unwell, when the money is gone, when the structures collapse, when the judgments are the most negative. Praises to those empathic people who can see past our circumstances to our divine nature. Where would we be without our rainy day people? Try to imagine a world without them. Kudos to those who make a point of supporting others in their time of need.

I am glad you were born. Such an important thing
to say, but so seldom heard. I wonder what would
happen on this planet if we said it to each other
on a regular basis. Even to seeming strangers we
encounter on our daily travels. I am glad you were
born—the anti-shame mantra. I am glad you were
born. I am glad you were born. I am glad...

It is one thing to make a determined effort to excavate and actualize our sacred purpose, but quite another to seek perfection. In many ways, perfectionism is the anti-thesis of spiritual expansion and an obstacle on the path. We are not striving to become perfect. We are striving to become real, to show up for our life in every respect.

We are powerful beyond measure, and so deeply vulnerable at the same time. This may seem like a dichotomy, but it isn't. We have misunderstood real power. It has been something assertive, non-surrendering, pushing on through. This is not real power. This is simply willfulness. Real power is something else—receptivity, open-ness, the courage to keep your heart open on the darkest of days, the strength to feel it all even when the odds are stacked against you. Real power is showing up with your heart on your sleeve and absolutely refusing to waste one moment of your life hidden behind edginess and armour. The art of enheartened presence. Now that's power.

What could be more beautiful than looking back at the end of your life and knowing that you did what you came here to do? Isn't this the way you want to close your eyes for the last time?

May we all realize how beautiful this life is before our eyes close on this incarnation.

Don't just follow your dreams. You may lose them at a red light, or while wandering the trailways of transformation. Better yet, ingest and embody them, make them indistinguishable from you. Weave your most wondrous imaginings into the breath of your being.

Apologies to The Divine Feminine

(from a warrior in transition)

I apologize for my inability to distinguish the benevolent warrior from the heartless warrior, a reflection of my own confusion dealing with the battlefields of yore. When I opened my heart too wide, I was vulnerable to attack from warring factions. I was conditioned to believe that I had to stay rigid, focused, prepared for any eventuality, in the desire to protect myself and others from attack. But I went too far, and closed too tight, and eradicated the bridge between our hearts. I am seeing this now and I am sorry.

I apologize for my perpetual absence, a reflection of my own inner absence, my inability to connect from a heart jammed tight by unresolved emotions that I did not have the tools to work through. I still lack many of these tools, but I am open to their emergence.

I apologize for my inability to distinguish relationship from war. Like a warrior in enemy territory, I would sneak in and out of your life in the night, plundering and selfishly taking what I needed, then crawling back to the other side of the abyss with the spoils. I gave little back for fear that I would become vulnerable to attack. I had war on the brain and I could not see the river of love waiting on the other side of the battlefield. I now recognize that love is the antidote for the armoured warrior, but I could not drink the antidote in my driven state.

I apologize for not seeing you, my eyes blinded by congealed rage and unshed tears. If it is any consolation, and I imagine it is not, I could not see myself either. I saw only that which served my hyper-vigilance, my warrior focus. My mirror was a battlefield.

I apologize for my ungrounded materialism, my power driven tyrannies, my obsession with accumulation. Somehow I imagined that accumulation would protect me and those close to me, but I failed to recognize that it just perpetuated the madness. I also apologize for my egoic abuses, a reflection of my own misguided ego, pumped up to deal with an inherently competitive world. I couldn't distinguish the healthy, confident ego from the cocky, unhealthy ego. I went much too far in the wrong direction.

I apologize for a sexuality that was objectifying and disconnected from the heart. I know you longed for real intimacy, a merging of our souls along the heart-genital highway. But there were too many defences around my heart, and no bridge could form between our souls. There were moments when your loving ways freed me from my body masks, but I had no template to stand in that heart-fire. I am sorry for this, for I know that the path you longed for was the path to God.

I apologize for my horrifying acts of violence, a reflection of my own congealed rage, my own inability to distinguish real enemies from friends. There are no words that can undo what I have done in those moments of madness. I know this, I do. I would hide my face in shame, but that won't make things better. I need to own my misdeeds, and then find a way to believe in my capacity to move from a more loving place. I call out to other male warriors to be accountable for the actions of our gender, not in a way that is self-hating, but in a way that is courageously self-honest and genuinely compassionate. The heartfelt warrior acknowledges the error of his ways, and has the courage to do all he can to make amends over time.

I apologize for my inability to develop a conscious relationship. You were right there with your beautiful heart on your sleeve but I was too attached to my individualism and afraid of this unknown terrain. I know the forests, the marketplace and the ways of the outer world so well, but my inner geography is foreign to me. You called me to a place I was ill-prepared to go, although I sensed, below the surface of my bravado, that you called me home.

I am grateful for your willingness to believe that who I was in those rare moments of vulnerability was the real me. You were right—the real me lives inside of my heart—but a few moments now and then was the most I could handle. I saw you as dangerous, for in your presence I began to taste a surrendered way of being. Nonetheless, your faith in my goodness kept me going through many a battle, and restored my faith in life when I most needed it. You were the light at the end of a barbaric tunnel, and I am blessed.

I am grateful that you stuck with me through thick and thin, and I also understand those times you had to give up and let go. I now recognize that there is a meaningful difference between a love-ship and a relationship. Love alone is not enough. Without a shared willingness to become conscious, there can only be frustration. I was so often impossible, clinging to my unconsciousness like a soldier clings to his weapons. I recognize the courage it took for you to keep your heart open in the presence of my resistance. You had every right to seek an authentic relationship, as your spirit was ignited in its presence. Your beautiful heart had every right to be met in its openness and willingness. I am grateful for the time you gave me, a moments respite from the hiding places I mistakenly called home.

I am grateful for Grandmother, for no one saw my tenderness more clearly. I am grateful for Mother, for choosing to bring me into being and for nourishing my body until I could find my feet. I am grateful for Mother Earth, for grounding my expansion and enlivening my spirit. I am grateful for the Divine Mother, the real

Mother of us all. I now feel her divine presence, so close. Fiercely compassionate, she was always right here, breathing life into me, holding me safe. I sit in her lap as she breathes me.

I look forward to the day when the only thing that ignites relationship is two souls calling out to one another, two soul-hearts beating in the same direction, a whisper of longing that bridges one essence to another. I want to want you not because it gratifies my ego, not because you are outwardly beautiful, but because your very presence invites my Godself out of hiding. I want to touch you with my heart on my sleeve, to know chemistry between us that is not gender identified, but that is essence sourced, love's liquid lava flowing from the heart to the genitals to the great beyond. In this love-struck world, relationship will always be experienced as spiritual practice, a devotional expression of our God-self.

I had always believed that sensitivity is impossible to hold to in a harsh world. Yet in this moment, I feel sensitive, but without the fragility. I am still wearing armor but there is a shift in the direction of my intensity. I can linger in the heart-space a little longer than I once could, I am softening in places. After so many lifetimes with weapon in hand, a tenderling warrior is being birthed in the core of my being. He is confused, but he intuitively knows that this is the way home.

Please don't give up on me or my fellow warriors. Forgive us our misdeeds, or, at the least, be open to the possibility that we will change as the trail expands to meet our shifting intentionality. The day will come when our warrior spirit loses its harsh edge, and comes into alignment with benevolent action. Some of us are already there, and many more of us will follow. The road to transformation is dependent on a bridge between genders, a benevolent bridge that celebrates our differences with respect and kindness. That work must begin with healing the rifts along the gender continuum, working hard to heal the collective heart until one day we can stand on a bridge across forever, hands held together, hearts open and alight, embracing the sacred masculine and divine feminine living at the heart of us all. I will meet you there.

May you feel the love of the Divine Mother crashing down on your heartfelt shores, graciously lifting you up above the madness of the world, nestling you in the grateful arms of those you have nurtured. Those of us who have received your blessings may not always acknowledge it, but your acts of love have landed within us, growing us stronger and infusing us with love's light. Thank you.

J. B., 2010
(originally published September 20th, 2010)

Apologies to The Sacred Masculine

(The letter this warrior-in-transition
would like to receive)

I apologize for those moments when I couldn't see beyond my projections to your true nature. With so much relational trauma in the rear view mirror, I couldn't distinguish the heartless from the benevolent warrior. With my lens blurred by unhealed emotions, I was unable to see you in your wholeness. I unknowingly projected my negative expectations without recognizing those moments when you were moving from love. Please forgive me my projections, and know that below my pain was a heart that genuinely longed to merge with yours.

I apologize for pushing you to open your heart when you weren't ready. I longed to be met in my openness, and I couldn't bear the disconnect between us. I am nourished by direct communication, and I took your silence personally. I didn't understand the relationship between your detachment and your warrior conditioning. I do see this now. From the beginning, you have been cast in the role of warrior protector and your emotional armour was fundamental to your task. Without it, you would not have been able to remain vigilant on the battlefield, nor succeed in the competitive marketplace.

As our world moves away from survivalism as a way of being, I am hopeful that you will feel safe enough to live from an open heart. Such beautiful light comes through that opening.

I apologize for not always seeing your limitations and struggles. There were times when I could not see past my expectations and fantasies. I had grown up with a fairy tale of a great knight that would save me, and I clung to that vision, preferring the perfection projection to the reality of humanness. As a result, I didn't always see how much stress you carried, how difficult things were, how hard it was to hold it all together. Of course, we perpetuated the projection together—you hid your humanness from view while I chose not to look for it. I look forward to the day when our relationships are not predicated on illusions, but on a deep recognition of each other's authenticity.

I apologize for giving you mixed messages about how I wanted you to manifest. At times, I wanted you to be soft and tender. At other times, dominant and protect-ive. How confusing this must have been for you, how challenging to go back and forth between such differing feeling states. It has been so confusing for all of us, try-ing to straddle the line between our needs for both safety and vulnerability. One day, the perversions of polarity will fall away and we will arrive at a sacred balance between all healthy ways of being. Women will feel safe to assert their voice and embody their wholeness, and men will feel equally safe disarming and speaking from their vulnerability. On the rivers of essence, everything flows in the same direction—towards the ocean of wholeness.

I apologize for being passive aggressive towards you. I was not taught to express anger directly, and I was frightened of your aggressiveness. I know that you have had similar challenges with experiencing your sadness and releasing your tears. In the world we are moving towards, I am hopeful that both genders will have seamless access to all emotional states and healthy forms of expression.

I am sorry that I expected you to fill my emptiness, when the only one who can fill it is me. I have often looked for answers in relationship, somehow imagining that another could complete me. After so many centuries of disempowerment, I didn't realize that I had the tools for my own self-creation. But I am recognizing it now. Where before we met as two fragmented beings, we will soon meet as two whole beings—each of us healthily boundaried, well-integrated and intrinsically complete. Two soulitudes.

I am grateful for all those moments when you held me safe and operated within the heart of compassion. The backlash of recent decades was a necessary response to generations of suffering, but many of your contributions got lost in the shuffle. In my efforts to find my voice and stand my ground, I have not always given credit where it is due. I encourage you to re-claim anything you have lost along the way, and to proudly embody the sacred masculine as you once did. I apologize for those moments when I discouraged your power. I could not distinguish it from its historical misuses.

I am grateful for the many positive contributions you have made to my reality. I realize that you often communicated your love for me and the village with deeds, not words. I thank you for helping to construct the structures that my expansion relies upon. I thank you for labouring long and hard to establish rule of law. I honour the warrior spirit that built the railroads, the cities, the bridges that bring us into contact with one another. I honour those warriors who fought and died on battlefields in an effort to protect us. You have sacrificed so much in order to hold us safe. Praise to those benevolent warriors who came before.

I am grateful for GrandFather, for holding the space for my expansion with patience and wisdom. I am grateful for Father, for defending and sheltering me. I am grateful for Father Sky, for showing me a vision of possibility that transcended my circumstances. I am grateful for the Divine Father, the real Father of us all. I now feel his divine presence, so close. Fiercely compassionate, he was always right here, holding me safe.

There has been so much blame between us, so much hatred and name-calling. To be sure, it is essential that we express our anger and heal our hearts. Nothing should be swept under the rug in that process, everything should be exposed. But it is also important that we have compassion for each other and endeavour to understand the context for our actions. We have all been victims of a sociological landscape that impacted on our identifications and behaviours. Like two different species in the same bed, we were compelled by circumstances to inhabit roles that kept us miles apart. Those roles have caused us great suffering, each gender suffering in its own way. To the extent that one gender was denied wholeness, the other was denied it as well. Women were denied the right to basic protections and pathways of expression, men were denied access to a tender, receptive way of being. No one got off easy, despite appearances.

As we move towards a more enheartened interface, may we create space for new visions of possibility. We must begin the process by healing the genderation gap that exists between us. We must soften the edges perpetuated by our reactivities. We must heal the rifts along the gender continuum that keep us apart. In my most clarified imaginings, I envision a world that fully celebrates the healthy feminine and the healthy masculine. Instead of throwing all gender differences out with the bath water, we make a conscious distinction between benevolent and destructive identifications. We craft a sacred balance of our healthiest aspects. Each of us identifies the unique fusion of feminine and masculine energies that aligns with our essential nature. And we openly learn from one another -men teach healthy manifestation, women teach healthy womanifestation—and we come to humanifestation together. We meet each other in our entirety.

May we never forget the relational and co-transformative nature of human expansion. Although the ultimate romance is with your own soul, it is our experiences together that give birth to the essential lessons. We are each here to participate in this dance of sacred imagination, stepping on each other's toes and turning each other toward God one clumsy step after another. We trip, and then we get back up with greater awareness. With this in heart, I am hopeful that we can learn to accept one another in our humanness. We are going to continue to make mistakes, but there is grace in that if we see our errors through to the lessons they contain.

I look forward to the day when we can meet one another in our true nakedness, stripped free of unresolved emotions, pain-induced projections, the distortions of duality. For too long we have been on opposite sides of the river, the bridge between our hearts washed away by a flood of pain. But the time has come to construct a new bridge, one that comes into being with each step we take, one that is fortified with benevolent intentions and authentic self-revealing. As we walk toward one another, our emotional armour falls to the ground, transforming into the light at its source. And when we are ready, we walk right into the Godself at the centre of the bridge, puzzled that we ever imagined ourselves separate.

May you feel the presence of the Divine Mother close at heart, inviting you to rest deeply on the tender shores of your own essence, nestling you in the grateful arms of those you have protected. Those who have received your blessings may not always acknowledge it, but your acts of love have landed within us, growing us stronger and infusing us with love's light. Rest dear warrior, rest. I hold your heart safe.

J. B., 2011
(originally published March 27th, 2011)

The Awakening Man

A Portrait of Possibility for Humankind

The awakening man is conscious, heartfully defined. Through his eyes, being conscious is not a cerebral construct, nor an intellectual exercise bereft of feeling. It is a felt experience, an ever-expanding awareness that moves from the heart outward. It is feeling God, not thinking God. The new man is always in process, awakening through a deepening interface with the world of feeling. He continues to strive for a more heartfelt and inclusive awareness.

The awakening man has shifted his focus from a localized and ethnocentric perspective to a world-centric framework of perception. His community is humanity. Rooted in the relational, his sense of responsibility extends well beyond his localized self and community. Where possible, his choice-making is fuelled by an expansive vision of possibility for all of humankind. Not every man for himself, but every man for humanity.

The awakening man has reverence for the divine feminine, in all her forms. He celebrates the wonder that is woman. He is respectful, honouring and gracious. He is saddened by the horrors perpetuated against women by the malevolent masculine. He holds his brothers accountable. He makes amends for his own misdeeds.

He co-creates a world where all women will feel safe to move about freely, to find their voice, to actualize their inherent magnificence. He welcomes a world where women and men stand as equal partners. Humankind.

The awakening man is not externally derived. He is authentically sourced. He does not compare himself to others. He does not adapt his personality to the dictates of the crowd. He stands in his own centre, respectful of others but not defined by them. He works diligently to liberate his consciousness from the egoic ties that bind. He has become his own benchmark, valuing authenticity over image. He is the sculptor of his own reality.

The awakening man courageously works on his emotional processes. He clears his emotional debris and sheds his armour. He faces his issues and unconscious patterns heart on. He calls himself on his self-avoidant tendencies and honours the wisdom at the heart of his pain. He communicates his feelings in a way that is respectful to others. He learns and speaks the language of the heart.

The awakening man leads a purpose-full existence. He has heard the call to a deeper life. Not satisfied with survival alone, his ambitions are rooted in higher considerations—the excavation and actualization of his sacred purpose. He is energized by his purpose, not by the machinations of the unhealthy ego. He is coated in an authenticity of purpose that sees through the veils to what really matters. His purpose is his path.

The awakening man is accountable for his actions and their effects. He does not deflect responsibility. He does not sidestep or blame. He is self-admitting and emotionally honest. He admits his errors, and makes amends. He works diligently in the deep within, crafting a more clarified awareness with every lesson.

The awakening man moves from the inside out. More interested in inner expansion than outer achievement, he cultivates and honours his intuition. He explores and develops his inner geography. He adventures deep within, integrating the treasures he excavates into his way of being. He seeks congruity between his inner life and his outer manifestation.

The awakening man seeks wholeness. He is not satisfied with a fragmented way of being. He has no attachment to archaic, linear notions of masculinity. He seeks a sacred balance between the healthy masculine and the healthy feminine. He seeks an inclusive way of being, one that reflects all of his archetypal aspects.

The awakening man embodies the highest standard of integrity in his words and deeds. He makes a sustained effort to work through anything that is not in integrity within him. His framework of integrity is never convenient or self-serving. He honours his word, even at his own expense. He moves from a value system that is unwaveringly incorruptible. He recognizes that success without integrity is karmically unsound and meaningless.

The awakening man prioritizes conscious relationship. He values authentic co-creation. He honours relationship as spiritual practice. He seeks physical intimacy that is deeply vulnerable and heartfully connective. He is attuned, engaged and healthily boundaried. When relational challenges arise, he courageously works through any obstructions to intimacy. He stands in the heartfire.

The awakening man is a warrior of the heart. He has taken his clarifying sword inward, cutting away everything that is not compassionate. After too many lifetimes with weapon in hand, a benevolent warrior is being birthed at the core of his being. He honours the warrior capacity for assertiveness, but he is not arbitrarily aggressive. He moves from love and compassion.

The awakening man endeavours to live in a state of perpetual gratitude. He is grateful for the gift of life. He is grateful for those ancestors who built the foundation that his expansion relies upon. He is grateful for those who encouraged him before he could encourage himself. He is grateful for those who stand beside him in this lifetime. He knows that he does not stand alone.

The awakening man is comfortable in his vulnerability. He participates in his own revealing. He is not afraid to surrender—to reality, to love, to truth. This is not a weakened form of surrender, but one that is emblazoned with courage. It takes more courage to surrender than to numb. He openly explores his capacities for receptivity and tenderness. He does not identify these capacities as distinctly feminine, but as whole human. He is strong enough at the core to live in a vast array of emotions.

The awakening man moves through the market-place responsibly, with a vigilant eye to the ways of the unhealthy ego. He is not opportunistic in a vacuum. He does not compete for competition's sake. He does not accumulate for the sake of accumulation. In charting his course, he is mindful of his impact on humanity. He is empowered but he does not exploit power. He derives his power from his connection to source, not from power over others. Where possible, he shares the abundance, gifting back to humanity. He works hard to bridge the world as it is with a world of divine possibility.

The awakening man has reverence for Mother Earth. He has reverence for animals. He never imagines himself superior or distinct from the natural world. He understands the interconnected and interdependent nature of reality. He knows that if he does damage to the environment, he does damage to himself. He walks carefully, with awareness, consciousness and appreciation.

The awakening man has no claims on God. His spirituality is tolerant, inclusive, respectful. He honours all paths to God, so long they are respectful of others. He accepts those who believe, and those who don't. He condemns any path that uses religious differences as a justification for destruction.

The awakening man brings forward many of the qualities of the healthy masculine of old. He is noble. He is responsible. He is productive. He is kind-hearted. He is protective. He is unswervingly honourable. He is down to earth. He is sturdy. He is flexible. He is realistic. He is hopeful. He is sensitive, not fragile. He is healthily egoic, not self-centred. He is both practical and heightened at the same time. He ascends with both feet on the ground. He is really *here*.

J. B., 2011
(originally published June 30, 2011)

About the Author

Born in Toronto, Canada in 1962, Jeff Brown did all the things he was supposed to do to become successful in the eyes of the world. He was on the Dean's Honor List as an undergraduate. He won the Law and Medicine prize in law school. He apprenticed with top criminal lawyer Eddie Greenspan. It had been Brown's lifelong dream to practice criminal law and search for the truth in the courtroom.

But then, on the verge of opening a law practice, he heard a little voice inside telling him to stop, just stop. With great difficulty, he honored this voice and began a heartfelt quest for the truth that lived within him. Although he didn't realize it at the time, Brown was actually questing for his innate image, the essential being that he came into this lifetime to embody. He was searching for his authentic face.

As part of his journey, Brown explored many possible paths. He studied Bioenergetics and did session work with cofounder Alexander Lowen. He practiced as a body-centered psychotherapist and completed an MA in Psychology at Saybrook Graduate School in San Francisco. He also co-founded the *Open Heart Gang*, a benevolent gang with a heartfelt intention. Their first creation—the unforgettable spiritual documentary "Karmageddon"—is now completed.

In 2001, Jeff was overwhelmed by the need to write. It was strong and it was determined, a soulnami of sacred purpose that absolutely had to be expressed if he was to have any peace. This is in the nature of a calling once it has been awakened. After six years of hard work, his first book—*Soulshaping: Adventures in Self-Creation*—was published in 2007. With the help of a homeless man who sold the book on the streets of Toronto, Jeff's first press run quickly sold out. The book was then picked up by North Atlantic Books and published in August, 2009 with a new sub-title—*Soulshaping: A Journey of Self-Creation.*

Soon thereafter, Jeff began writing inspirations for ABC's Good Morning America. He was interviewed by CNN radio, appeared on Fox News.com, and wrote pieces for the Washington Post's On Faith blog and Insight Magazine.

In September, 2010, Jeff wrote a blog called *Apologies to the Divine Feminine—from a warrior in transition*, which was met with a viral response on Facebook and beyond. Since then, *Apologies* has been translated and re-printed countless times. That blog and two other popular blogs—*Apologies to the Sacred Masculine*, and *The Awakening Man*—are re-printed at the back of this book.

At present, Jeff is living just outside of Toronto, where he is writing and promoting Karmageddon (www.karmageddonthemovie.com). The film, which focuses on Jeff's 2005 journey with chanter and spiritual teacher Bhagavan Das, includes wonderful interviews with Jeff and author Ram Dass, yogis Seane Corn and David Newman, and chanters Robert Gass, Wah, Deva Premal and Miten.

WWW.SOULSHAPING.COM